Hector Berlioz

SYMPHONIE FANTASTIQUE
AND
HAROLD IN ITALY
in Full Score

From the Complete Works Edition

Edited by
Charles Malherbe
and Felix Weingartner

DOVER PUBLICATIONS, INC.
New York

CONTENTS

PROGRAMME OF THE SYMPHONIE FANTASTIQUE

A young musician of unhealthily sensitive nature and endowed with vivid imagination has poisoned himself with opium in a paroxysm of love-sick despair. The narcotic dose he had taken was too weak to cause death but it has thrown him into a long sleep accompanied by the most extraordinary visions. In this condition his sensations, his feelings and memories find utterance in his sick brain in the form of musical imagery. Even the beloved one takes the form of melody in his mind, like a fixed idea which is ever returning and which he hears everywhere.

1st MOVEMENT. Visions and Passions.

At first he thinks of the uneasy and nervous condition of his mind, of sombre longings, of depression and joyous elation without any recognisable cause, which he experienced before the beloved one had appeared to him. Then he remembers the ardent love with which she suddenly inspired him; he thinks of his almost insane anxiety of mind, and his raging jealousy, of his re-awakening love, of his religious consolation.

2nd MOVEMENT. A Ball.

In a ball-room, amidst the confusion of a brilliant festival, he finds the loved one again.

3rd MOVEMENT. In the Country.

It is a summer evening. He is in the country musing when he hears two shepherd-lads who play the *ranz des vaches* (the tune used by the Swiss to call their flocks together) in alternation. This shepherd-duet, the locality, the soft whisperings of the trees stirred by the zephyr-wind, some prospects of hope recently made known to him, all these sensations unite to impart a long unknown repose to his heart and to lend a smiling color to his imagination. And then she appears once more. His heart stops beating, painful forebodings fill his soul. "Should she prove false to him!" One of the shepherds resumes the melody, but the other answers him no more. . . . Sunset . . . distant rolling of thunder . . . loneliness . . . silence.

4th MOVEMENT. The Procession to the Stake.

He dreams that he had murdered his beloved, that he has been condemned to death and is being led to the stake. A march that is alternately sombre and wild, brilliant and solemn, accompanies the procession. . . . The tumultuous outbursts are followed without modulation by measured steps. At last the fixed idea returns, for a moment a last thought of love is revived—which is cut short by the death-blow.

5th MOVEMENT. The Witches' Sabbath.

He dreams that he is present at a witches' dance, surrounded by horrible spirits, amidst sorcerers and monsters in many fearful forms, who have come to attend his funeral. Strange sounds, groans, shrill laughter, distant yells, which other cries seem to answer. The beloved melody is heard again but it has its noble and shy character no longer; it has become a vulgar, trivial and grotesque kind of dance. *She* it is who comes to attend the witches' meeting. Friendly howls and shouts greet her arrival. . . . She joins the infernal orgy . . . bells toll for the dead . . . a burlesque parody of the *Dies irae* . . . the witches' round-dance . . . the dance and the *Dies irae* are heard at the same time.

Published in Canada by General Publishing Company, Ltd., 30 Lesmill Road, Don Mills, Toronto, Ontario.
Published in the United Kingdom by Constable and Company, Ltd.

This Dover edition, first published in 1984, is an unabridged republication of the music of Nos. 1 and 3 of *Serie I. Symphonien* (1900) of *Werke von Hector Berlioz*, originally published by Breitkopf & Härtel, Leipzig, 1900–1910.

The publisher is grateful to the Sibley Music Library of the Eastman School of Music, Rochester, N.Y., for making its material available for reproduction.

Manufactured in the United States of America
Dover Publications, Inc., 31 East 2nd Street, Mineola, N.Y. 11501

Library of Congress Cataloging in Publication Data

Berlioz, Hector, 1803–1869.
  [Symphonie fantastique]
  Symphonie fantastique ; and, Harold in Italy.

  Originally published: Leipzig : Breitkopf & Härtel, 1900–1910.
  1. Symphonies—Scores. 2. Viola with orchestra—Scores. I. Malherbe, Charles. II. Weingartner, Felix, 1863–1942. III. Berlioz, Hector, 1803–1869. Harold en Italie. 1984. IV. Title: Symphonie fantastique. V. Title: Harold in Italy.
M1001.B53 op. 14 1984   83-20608
ISBN 0-486-24657-4

SYMPHONIE FANTASTIQUE, OP. 14

I.

Rêveries. Passions.   Visions and Passions.

*) Les onze mesures qui suivent sont d'une extrême difficulté; je ne saurais trop recommander aux chefs d'Orchestre de les faire répéter plusieurs fois et avec le plus grand soin, en commençant au changement de mouvement (Più mosso) et finissant à la rentrée du thème (I. tempo). Il sera bon de faire étudier leur trait aux 1ers et 2mes Violons séparément d'abord, puis avec le reste de l'Orchestre, jusqu'à ce qu'ils soient parfaitement sûrs de toutes les nuances de mouvement, qui me paraissent ce qu'il y a de plus difficile à obtenir de la masse, avec l'ensemble et la précision convenables. (Note de H. Berlioz.)

Die folgenden 11 Takte sind von aussergewöhnlicher Schwierigkeit; ich kann dem Dirigenten nicht genug empfehlen, sie mehrmals und mit der grössten Sorgfalt vom Wechsel des Zeitmasses (Più mosso) bis zum Wiedereintritt des Themas (Tempo I) zu wiederholen. Es wird gut sein, diese Stelle zuerst mit den 1.u.2.Violinen allein und nachher mit dem übrigen Orchester zu studiren, bis sie mit allen Abstufungen des Zeitmaasses vollkommen vertraut sind, was mir mit der nöthigen Übereinstimmung und Genauigkeit von einer Menge von Spielern am schwersten zu erreichen scheint.

The following 11 bars are of unusual difficulty. I cannot sufficiently advise the conductor to repeat them, and with the greatest care, from the change in time (Più mosso) to the resumption of the theme (Tempo I⁰). It is a good plan to take this passage at first with the violins (1⁰ and 2⁰) only and afterwards with the rest of the orchestra until they are perfectly familiar with all grades of the tempo, which seems to me to be the most difficult to obtain with the necessary unity and exactness from a number of players.

Allegro agitato e appassionato assai. ($\flat$ = 132.)

Une mesure de ce mouvement équivaut au quart de la précédente.
Ein Takt dieses Zeitmaasses wie ein Viertel des vorhergehenden.
One bar of this time-measure is equal to a quarter-bar of the preceding movement.

cresc. ed un poco string.

cresc. ed un poco string.

Baguettes d'éponge.
Schwammschlägel.
Sponge-headed drum-sticks.

poco ritenuto

poco ritenuto

Baguettes d'éponge.
Schwammschlägel.
Sponge-headed drum-sticks.

Viole div.

Vcelli. unis.

C. B.

poco più lento

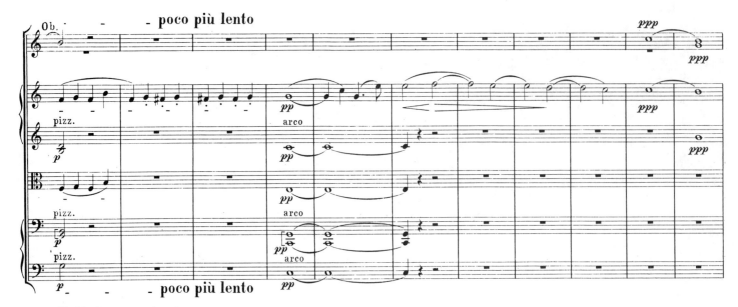

Religiosamente.

Tout l'orchestre aussi doux que possible.
Das ganze Orchester so zart als möglich.
The whole orchestra as soft as possible.

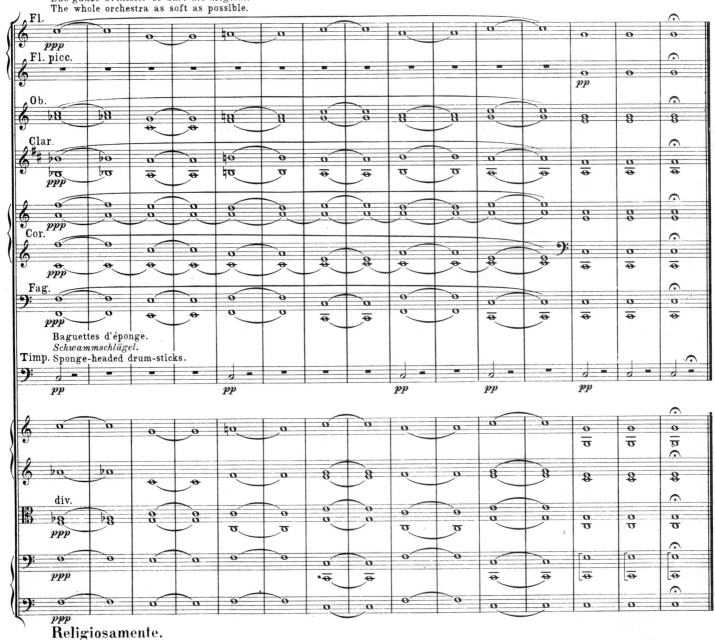

Religiosamente.

II.
Un Bal. A Ball.

VALSE. Allegro non troppo. (♩.=60.)

2 Flauti.
Flauto II =Flauto piccolo.

Oboe.

2 Clarinetti in A (*La*).

I.II. in E (*Mi*).
4 Corni.
III.IV. in C (*Ut*).

*) **Cornetto in A** (*La*).
(Cornet a pistons.)

Arpa I.

Arpa II.

Violino I.

Violino II.

Viola.

Violoncello.

Contrabasso.

VALSE. Allegro non troppo. (♩.=60.)

Arpa I.

Arpa II.

Viol.

cresc. poco a poco

cresc. poco a poco

cresc. poco a poco

*) Diese Stimme ist von Berlioz im Autograph später hinzugefügt worden. Die Herausgeber empfehlen, sie wegzulassen.
Cette partie se trouve sur l'autographe et a été ajoutée par Berlioz plus tard. Les éditeurs recommandent de l'omettre.
This part has been later added by Berlioz himself in the autograph. The editors recommend to omit same.

*) Le signe ‿ indique qu'il faut traîner le son d'une note à l'autre. (H. Berlioz.)

Das Zeichen ‿ bedeutet, dass der Ton von einer Note zur andern herabgezogen werden soll.

The sign ‿ indicates that the tone should be drawn down from one note to the other.

rallent.   Tempo I. con fuoco.

III.

Scène aux champs. In the country.

Le Hautbois rentre à l'orchestre.
Der Hoboist geht in das Orchester zurück.
The Oboe-player returns to the orchestra.

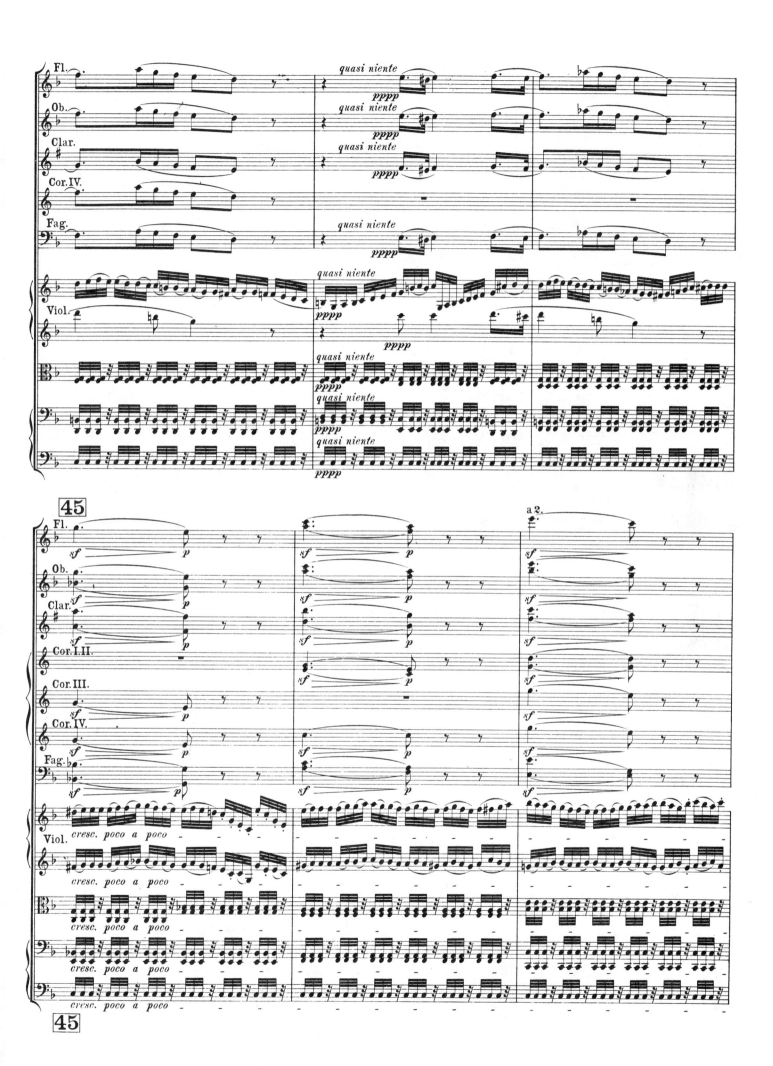

IV.

Marche au Supplice.   The Procession to the Stake.

*) On peut, dans ce morceau, doubler les instruments à vent. (Note de H. Berlioz.)
In diesem Satz können die Blasinstrumente verdoppelt werden.
In this movement the wind-instruments may be doubled.

senza sordini*)
Baguettes de bois.
Holzschlägel.
Wooden drum-sticks.

senza sordini*)
Baguettes de bois.
Holzschlägel.
Wooden drum-sticks.

*) Diese Anmerkung lässt darauf schliessen, dass der Componist die Pauken zu Anfang dieses Stückes con sordini (coperti) haben wollte.

Anm. d. Herausgeber.

Cette indication permet de supposer que le compositeur voulait avec sourdines les timbales au commencement de ce morceau.

Note des éditeurs.

This remark leads to the conclusion that the composer desired the kettle-drums to be muffled at the beginning of this piece.

Note by the Editors.

*) Il n'y a pas de faute de copie ici; c'est bien l'accord de Sol naturel mineur qui froisse de très près l'accord de Ré bémol majeur; l'auteur recommande aux Violons et Altos de ne pas «corriger» leurs parties en mettant des ♭ aux Ré, quintes de l'accord de Sol. (Note de H. Berlioz.)

Hier ist kein Schreibfehler; der G moll-Akkord steht unmittelbar neben dem Des dur-Akkord. Der Componist ersucht die Violinisten und Bratschisten, ihre Stimmen nicht durch Vorsetzen eines ♭ zum D, der Quinte des G moll-Akkordes, zu „corrigiren".

This is no clerical error; the G-minor-chord is immediately neat to the D-flat-major chord. The composer requests the violinists and violaplayers not to "correct" their parts by placing a ♭ before the D of the fifth of the G-minor-chord.

V

Songe d'une nuit du Sabbat.   A witches' sabbath.

Si l'on ne peut trouver deux Cloches assez graves pour sonner l'un des trois UT et l'un des trois SOL qui sont écrits, il vaut mieux employer des Pianos. Ils exécuteront alors la partie de Cloche en double octave, comme elle est écrite. (Note de H. Berlioz.)

Kann man nicht zwei Glocken finden, welche gross genug sind, um eines der drei C und eines der drei G, die vorgeschrieben sind, erklingen zu lassen, so ist es besser, die Klaviere zu verwenden. Man spielt dann die Glockenpartie in doppelter Octave, so wie sie geschrieben ist.

If 2 bells are not available which are large enough to produce one of the 3 Cs and one of the 3 Gs as written, it is better to use the piano-fortes. In such event the bell-part must be played with double-octaves as written.

*) Die Herausgeber empfehlen, die folgenden Takte auf fünfsaitigen Contrabässen in der tiefen Octave zu spielen.
Les mesures suivantes se jouent une octave plus bas sur la contrebasse à 5 cordes. (Note des Éditeurs.)
The editor wishes the following bars to be played on a 5-stringed double-bass in the lower octave.

Dies iræ.
senza accel.

senza accel.

Ronde du Sabbat.
Witches' round dance.
Poco meno mosso.*)

Poco meno mosso.

*) Le mouvement, qui a dû s'animer un peu, redevient ici comme au chiffre ⬚63⬚ Allegro (♩.= 104)
Das Zeitmaass, welches sich etwas belebt hat, wird hier wieder wie bei Ziffer ⬚63⬚ Allegro (♩.= 104)
The movement, which has animated itself, is here again as at number ⬚63⬚ Allegro (♩.= 104)

Dies irae et Ronde du Sabbat (ensemble).
Dies irae and witches' round dance (together).

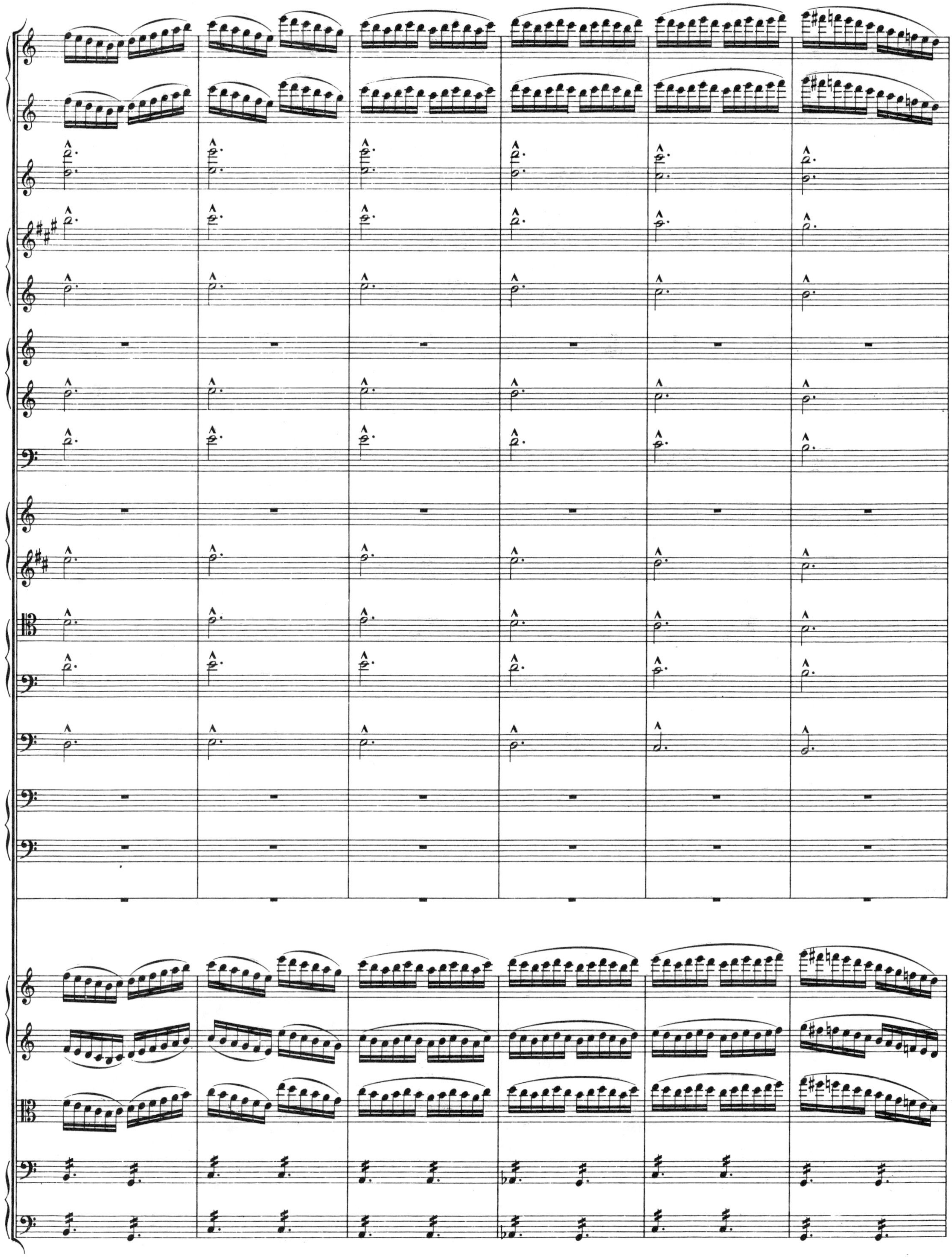

poco animato

Coup frappé sur une Cymbale avec une baguette
couverte d'éponge ou un tampon.
Schlag auf ein Becken mit einem Schwamm-
schlägel oder Klöppel.
Struck on a cymbal with a sponge-headed
drum-stick.

Cinelli.

HAROLD IN ITALY, OP. 16

I.

Harold aux Montagnes.
Scènes de mélancolie, de bonheur et de joie.

Harold in the Mountains.
Scenes of melancoly. happiness and joy.

poco più mosso

poco più mosso (♩.=120)

Ici le mouvement doit être devenu, peu à peu, presque du double plus animé qu'au commencement de l'Allegro. (Note de H. Berlioz.)
Hier muss das Zeitmaass nach und nach um das Doppelte gegen den Anfang gesteigert worden sein.
Here the tempo must be gradually increased to about the double of that at the beginning.

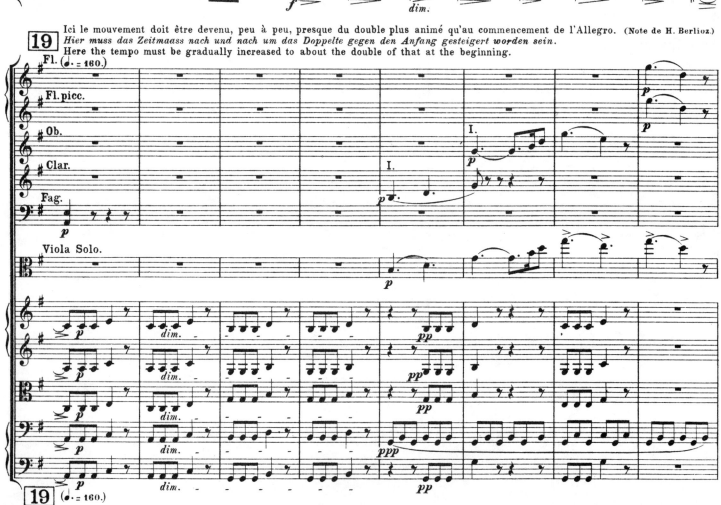

II.

Marche de pèlerins
chantant la prière du soir.

Procession of pilgrims
singing the evening hymn.

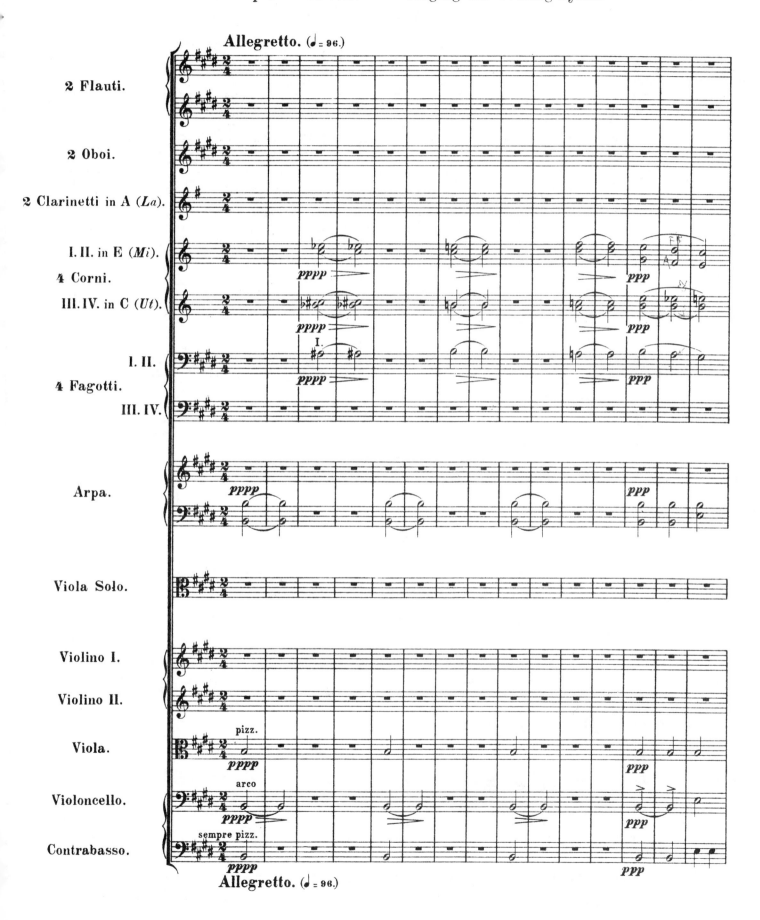

Il faut observer un *crescendo* extrèmement ménagé depuis 20 jusqu'à 26 où le *forte* doit se faire sentir complètement pour la première fois et, observant la progression inverse, aller en *diminuant* graduellement depuis 26 jusqu'à la fin, de manière cependant à atteindre le *pianissimo général* dès 31. (Note de H. Berlioz.) *)

Man achte auf ein äusserst mässiges Crescendo von 20 bis 26, wo das Forte *zum erstenmal voll zur Geltung kommt, und umgekehrt auf ein allmähliges* Diminuendo *von 26 bis zum Schluss; jedoch muss von 31 ab das* grösste Pianissimo *eingehalten werden.* *)

The *crescendo* from 20 to 26, where the *forte* must take full effect, must be extremely moderate. This effect must be reversed, namely a very gradual *decrescendo* must begin at 26 and be continued to the end, nevertheless from 31 onwards, the softest *possible pianissimo* must be maintained. *)

Le *diminuendo* commence ici; mais il ne doit devenir apparent qu'à 27 .
Das Diminuendo *beginnt hier, darf aber vor* 27 *kaum bemerkbar werden.*
The *diminuendo* begins here, but it must hardly be perceptible before 27 .
(Note de H.B.)

(poco a poco dim.)

III.

Sérénade
d'un Montagnard des Abruzzes à sa maîtresse.

Serenade
of an Abruzzi-mountaineer to his sweetheart.

Une mesure de ce mouvement équivaut à deux du mouvement précédent.
Jeder Takt gleichwerthig zwei Takten des vorhergehenden Zeitmaasses.
Each bar of this part is equal in time-value to two of the preceding ones.

Allegretto. (♩.= 69.)

Le double moins vite.
Doppelt so langsam.
Twice as slowly.

Pendant ces deux premières mesures, le chef d'orchestre marquera quatre temps par mesure, deux en bas et deux en haut.
Während dieser zwei ersten Takte gibt der Dirigent vier Schläge für jeden Takt, zwei nach unten und zwei nach oben.
During these two first bars the conductor to give four beats to each bar, two downwardo and two upwards.

Ici il ne marquera que les deux temps du mouvement lent.
Von hier ab gibt er nur noch die zwei Schläge des langsamen Zeitmaasses.
From here onwards he is only to give the two beats of the slow time-measure.

Les altos conservent le même mouvement.
Die Bratschen bleiben im gleichen Zeitmaass(Allegro assai).
The violas retain the same tempo (allegro assai.)

Allegretto. (♩.= 69.)

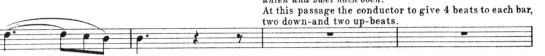

Ici le chef d'orchestre marquera 4 temps dans chaque mesure: deux temps en bas et deux en haut.
*Hier gibt der Dirigent **4** Schläge in jedem **Takt**, zwei nach
unten und zwei nach oben.*
At this passage the conductor to give 4 beats to each bar,
two down-and two up-beats.

Marquez seulement les deux temps du mouvement lent.
Nur zwei Schläge des langsamen Tempo geben.
Only two beats of the slow tempo to be given here.

IV.

Orgie de Brigands.
Souvenirs des scènes précédentes.

The brigand's Orgies.
Reminiscences of the preceding scenes.

Souvenir de l'introduction.
Erinnerung an die Einleitung.
A reminiscence of the introduction.

Adagio. (♪ = 76.)

Souvenir de la marche des pélerins.
Erinnerung an den Pilgerzug.
A reminiscence of the pilgrims' procession.
L'istesso tempo.

Souvenir de la sérénade du montagnard.
Erinnerung an die Serenade des Bergbewohners.
A reminiscence of the mountaineer's Serenade.

Même valeur de mesure. Le Chef d'orchestre marquera trois temps jusqu'au *fortissimo.*
Dieselbe Dauer der Takte. Der Dirigent gibt drei Schläge bis zum Fortissimo.
The bars have the same time-value. The conductor to give three beats (to a bar) up to the *fortissimo.*

38 poco ritenuto il tempo

poco ritenuto il tempo

38

Souvenir du premier Allegro.
Erinnerung an das erste Allegro.
A reminiscence of the first Allegro.

Souvenir de l'Adagio.
Erinnerung an das Adagio.
A reminiscence of the Adagio.

Ce roulement se fait avec les doigts.
Dieser Wirbel wird mit den Fingern gemacht.
This roll to be produced with the fingers.

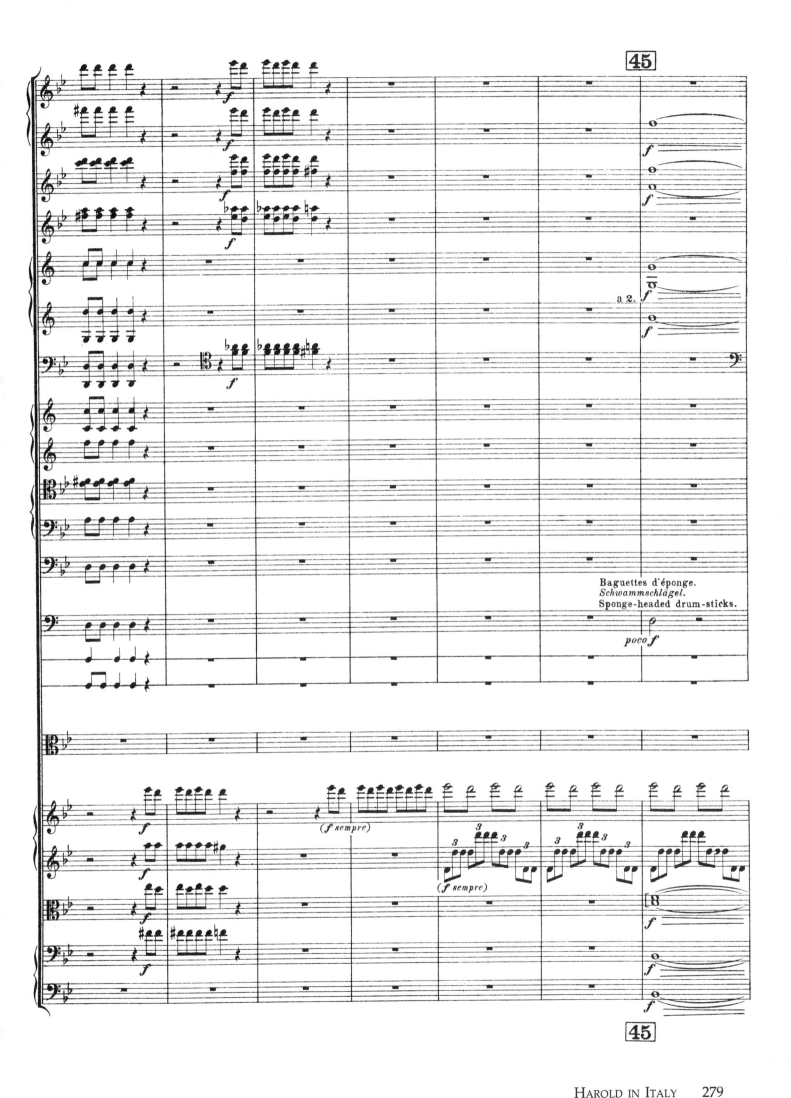

Baguettes de bois.
Holzschlägel.
Wooden-headed drum-sticks.

Ce roulement se fait avec les doigts.
Dieser Wirbel wird mit den Fingern gemacht.
This roll to be produced with the fingers.

senza accelerando

senza accelerando

Baguettes d'éponge.
Schwammschlägel.
Sponge-headed drum-sticks.

302   HAROLD IN ITALY

Le chef d'orchestre marquera trois temps dans la mesure, sans ralentir.
Der Dirigent gibt drei Schläge für jeden Takt, ohne zurückzuhalten.
The conductor to give three beats each bar, without relaxing the tempo.

Il reprendra ici la mesure à 2 temps.
Hier gibt er wieder 2 Schläge.
Resume here 2 beats to a bar.

(Roulement avec les doigts.)
(Wirbel mit den Fingern.)
(Roll with the fingers.)

marquez les trois temps
3 Schläge geben
three beats to a bar

marquez deux temps
2 Schläge geben
two beats to a bar

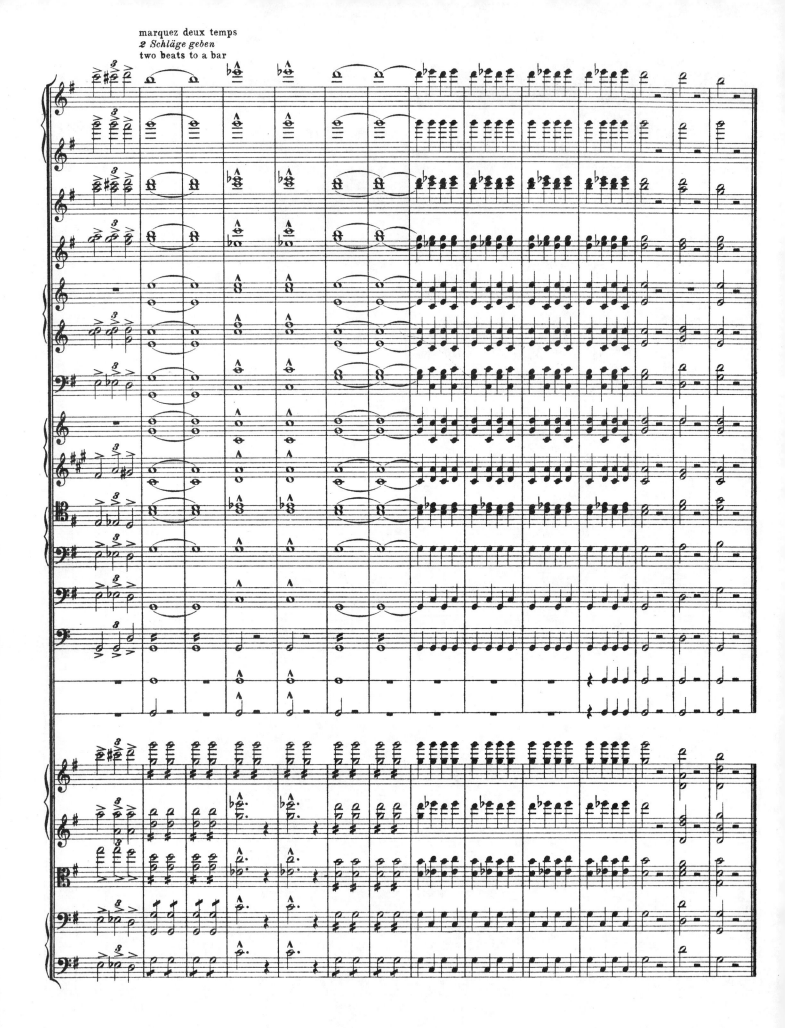